VELOCITY OF HOPE:
The Duke's Voyage to Fulfillment

ONESIMUS MALATJI

Copyright © 2023 ONESIMUS MALATJI

All rights reserved.

Velocity of Hope

VELOCITY OF HOPE: THE DUKE'S VOYAGE TO FULFILLMENT
By: Onesimus Malatji

Copyright ©2023 by Onesimus Malatji

Cover Design by CiX Connect
Interior Design by CiX Connect

Trademark Notice:

All trademarks mentioned within this book belong to their respective owners.

All rights reserved. No part of this publication may be reproduced, distributed, or transmitted in any form or by any means, including photocopying, recording, or other electronic or mechanical methods, without the prior written permission of the publisher, except in the case of brief quotations embodied in critical reviews and certain other non-commercial uses permitted by copyright law.

For permissions requests, contact the publisher at:
ony@cixconnect.co.za

Copyright Violation Warning:

Unauthorized reproduction or distribution of copyrighted material is against the law. Any unauthorized copying, distribution, or use of material from this book may result in legal action.
Fair Use Notice: This book may contain copyrighted material used for educational and illustrative purposes. Such material is used under the "fair use" provisions of copyright law.

Disclaimer:

The information provided in this book is for general informational purposes only. The author and publisher are not offering legal, financial, or professional advice. Readers are advised to consult appropriate professionals for advice specific to their individual situations.

Accuracy Disclaimer: While every effort has been made to ensure the accuracy of the information presented in this book, the author and publisher cannot be held responsible for any errors, omissions, or inaccuracies.

Fair Use Notice:

This book may contain copyrighted material used for educational and illustrative purposes. Such material is used under the "fair use" provisions of copyright law.

Third-Party Content:

This book may reference or include content from third-party sources. The author and publisher do not endorse or take responsibility for the accuracy or content of such third-party material.

Endorsements:

Any endorsement, testimonial, or representation contained in this book reflects the author's personal views and opinions. It does not imply an endorsement by any third party.
Results Disclaimer: The success stories and examples mentioned in this book are not guarantees of individual success. Actual results may vary based on various factors, including effort and circumstances.

Results Disclaimer:

The success stories and examples mentioned in this book are not guarantees of individual success. Actual results may vary based on various factors, including effort and circumstances.
No Guarantee of Outcome: The strategies, techniques, and advice provided in this book are based on the author's experiences and research. However, there is no guarantee that following these strategies will lead to a specific outcome or result.

Fair Use Notice:

This book may contain copyrighted material used for educational and illustrative purposes. Such material is used under the "fair use" provisions of copyright law.

DEDICATION

Being one of the difficulties in my family, always stubborn, I thank God I turned out alright. I dedicate this book to my mother, Esther Malatji. I will always love you. You have raised me well until I became a fully grown man. Thank you for your prayers and support during my tough times in life. Additionally, I extend my heartfelt dedication to my beautiful wife, the partner of my life, Petunia. You have been there for me and our family, and you are truly one in a million – the best motivator. I thank God for having you as my spouse, partner, and my inspiration; you are one of my most special and wonderful gifts. During times of trials, you have never walked out on us. Thank you. I love you so much.

I also send this dedication to my brother Edward "Gong," one of the greatest creative businesspersons alive. Thank you for being a wonderful brother and supporting me in times of need and trial. May God bless you and increase your business anointing. I love you so much. Special greetings to my sister Bertha, your passion for food will undoubtedly touch the world. I love you.

Furthermore, I extend my love and dedication to my brother Mohau; I will always cherish you, brother. Special Dedication for Galetsang & Dineo I will always love you no matter what. This is also for my friends, and fellow soldiers in war: Zama, Panana, Fina, Tshwane, Blessing, Lowen, Neo, I love you guys – you are my family. Special Gratitude to my inspirer my mother. I deeply respect the gift that God has put in you, and I am immensely grateful for having you while I was putting this book together.

Thank you, my dear mother, Esther Malatji. I love you so much

ACKNOWLEDGMENTS

I extend my deepest gratitude to everyone who has been a part of this incredible journey, both seen and unseen. Your support, encouragement, and unwavering belief in me have been the driving force behind the creation of this book.

To my family, for standing by me through thick and thin, for believing in my dreams, and for being a constant source of inspiration – your love and encouragement have been my guiding light. To my friends, mentors, and colleagues, your valuable insights and feedback have shaped the ideas within these pages. Your willingness to share your wisdom and experiences has enriched this work beyond measure.

To all those who have supported me on my path, whether through a kind word, a helping hand, or a moment of shared understanding, thank you. Your presence in my life has made all the difference. To the countless individuals who have faced challenges and setbacks, yet continued to strive for greatness, your stories have fueled the inspiration behind these words. May you find solace and encouragement within these pages.

And finally, to the readers who have embarked on this journey with me, thank you for allowing me to share my thoughts and experiences. It is my hope that this book serves as a beacon of hope, a source of guidance, and a reminder that fulfillment can be found in every step of life's intricate tapestry.

With heartfelt appreciation,

Onesimus "The Blender" Malatji

VELOCITY OF HOPE:
The Duke's Voyage to Fulfillment

TABLE OF CONTENTS	PAGES
Humble beginnings	8-10
Seeds of ambition	11-12
Crossroads of choices	13-15
The university bound	16-18
Bonds of friendship	19-20
The spark of love	21-23
Dreams unveiled	24-25
Tragedy strikes	26-28
Dark days	29-31
Unbreakable bonds	32-34
A parent's agony	35-37
The legal battle	38-40
Unveiling truths	41-43
The investigator's revelation	44-46
The turn of tides	47-49
The weight of acquittal	50-52
Healing wounds	53-55
Navigating relationships	56-58
A long road to recovery	59-61
The unseen hero	62-64
Rebuilding dreams	65-67
A parent's triumph	68-70
The birth of "duke"	71-73
Struggles of success	74-76
The motto	77-79
Unveiling the dream	80-82
Triumph of vision	83-85
Legacy forged	86-87
A new chapter	88-90
Merriam's choice	91-93
The winds of change	94-96
Julia's path	97-99
Abram's epiphany	100-102
The road ahead	103-105
The power of resilience	106-108
Bonds forever	109-111
Reflections	112-114
Full circle	115-117
Epilogue: echoes of dreams	118-120

HUMBLE BEGINNINGS

In the heart of bustling Johannesburg, a city that thrived on ambition and resilience, lived a couple whose story was a testament to both. Joseph and Tina were not born into luxury; they carved their path through grit and determination. Theirs was a tale of dreams nurtured in the shadows of uncertainty, dreams that bloomed into a reality beyond imagination.

Joseph, a man of rugged hands and an insatiable curiosity, began his journey in a modest garage. With little more than his skill and a toolbox, he embarked on a mission to mend broken engines and worn-out tires. Each wrench turns and each engine roar carried the echoes of his aspirations, painting the walls of his garage with stories of ambition.

Tina, his equal in spirit and a partner in every sense, complemented his dreams with a keen sense of business acumen. She meticulously managed the financial aspects of their enterprise, transforming it from a humble garage to a thriving automotive haven. The journey was not without its challenges, but their unity in purpose made them an unstoppable force.

South Africa provided the canvas upon which their story unfolded. The nation's vibrant landscapes mirrored the hues of their journey - from the rocky beginnings to the blooming prosperity. The rhythmic pulse of the city echoed their heartbeat, and the vistas stretching beyond Johannesburg's skyline whispered of boundless opportunities.

But their greatest masterpiece was their son, Duke. A boy with a name that carried weight, symbolizing nobility and destiny. From the moment he could string together thoughts, Duke's conversations revolved around one topic - cars. His eyes would light up at the mere mention of engines, his dreams fueled by the intricate mechanics and the allure of the open road.

Duke's room became a haven for his dreams, adorned with posters of iconic automobiles and shelves housing miniature replicas of his favourite cars. Late into the night, under the soft glow of a desk lamp, he would sketch designs that were a fusion of creativity and practicality. Each stroke of his pencil was a step closer to the world he yearned to shape.

In school, Duke was known as the "car enthusiast," a moniker he wore with pride. While his peers lost themselves in teenage fads, Duke lost himself in engine schematics and aerodynamics textbooks. His friends might not have understood the thrill of torque or the symphony of pistons, but Duke's passion was a fire that burned too bright to be extinguished.

As Joseph and Tina looked upon their son, they saw in him the embodiment of their own journey. They saw a dreamer, a young soul with a heart set on a course only he could see. They saw the baton of their ambition passing into the hands of the next generation, and they couldn't be prouder.

And so, against the backdrop of a rapidly changing South Africa, Joseph, Tina, and Duke stood as a testament to the power of dreams and the unbreakable bonds of family. Their humble beginnings were a foundation, and their shared aspirations would build a legacy that would resonate far beyond the city limits.

SEEDS OF AMBITION

As Duke stepped into his teenage years, the fire of his passion for cars burned brighter than ever. His weekends took on a new rhythm as he immersed himself in the world of automobiles. Local car shows became his sanctuary, a place where his dreams were fueled by the roar of engines and the sleek lines of expertly crafted vehicles.

With each visit to a car show, Duke found himself drawn to a different aspect of the automotive world. He marvelled at the precision of the engines, the artistry of the designs, and the innovation that breathed life into each vehicle. Amid the chrome and polished curves, he saw not just cars, but a canvas on which dreams were painted with the strokes of engineering brilliance.

His fascination went beyond the surface. Duke's keen eye caught the intricate details that made each car unique - the placement of the gears, the curvature of the fenders, the technology embedded within. He saw beyond the metal and rubber; he saw the heartbeat of ingenuity that turned raw materials into a symphony of motion.

Duke's conversations transformed as well. While his peers discussed music, movies, and trends, he delved into conversations about torque, horsepower, and suspension dynamics.

Velocity of Hope

He would passionately explain the difference between a V6 and a V8 engine, or how a rear-wheel-drive handled differently from a front-wheel-drive. His enthusiasm was infectious, and even those who weren't car enthusiasts found themselves captivated by his fervour.

In school, Duke's notebooks were a testament to his devotion. Scribbled equations and sketches of car parts adorned the margins, transforming his study materials into a blend of academia and passion. Teachers recognized his unique enthusiasm, and while some raised an eyebrow at his unconventional interests, many admired his dedication to his craft.

As he navigated the complexities of teenage life, Duke's passion provided him with a sense of purpose and identity. He wasn't just another student; he was a dreamer with aspirations that reached far beyond the confines of his classroom. Amid the hormonal tempest of adolescence, he found solace in the steady hum of engines and the steadfast pursuit of his ambitions.

Yet, as Duke's passion continued to flourish, he faced a crucial question: How could he turn his fervour for cars into a tangible path for his future? While the path ahead was uncertain, Duke carried with him the seeds of ambition that had taken root in his heart. Little did he know that these seeds would grow into a journey that would challenge him, transform him, and lead him closer to the realization of his dreams.

CROSSROADS OF CHOICES

High school graduation was on the horizon, casting a spotlight on Duke's journey thus far. Amidst the excitement of caps and gowns, a weighty decision loomed large in Duke's mind. The future, a tapestry of infinite possibilities, beckoned him to choose a path that would become the foundation of his destiny.

As college brochures piled up on his desk and guidance counsellors offered their insights, Duke's heart remained steadfast. Among the myriad of options, he held onto a dream that had never wavered - to study engineering and transform his car visions into tangible reality. His passion for automobiles had always burned fiercely within him, propelling him forward with an unstoppable force.

Amid the chatter of potential majors and the sway of well-intentioned advice, Duke found himself pausing to reflect on the words of his father, Joseph. It was Joseph who had fostered his love for cars, who had nurtured his curiosity about engines and mechanics. He had imparted to Duke the wisdom that success, no matter how grand, was rooted in pursuing one's passions.

Velocity of Hope

The world of engineering was a realm where Duke's dreams could take form. It was a pathway where the artistry of design and the precision of mechanics converged into a symphony of innovation. Engineering, he believed, would provide him with the tools to shape the vehicles that had fueled his imagination since childhood.

With resolute determination, Duke made his decision. The acceptance letters that arrived in the mail were more than just invitations to join prestigious institutions; they were affirmations of his dedication and the first steps toward his ultimate goal. As he prepared to embark on this new chapter, Duke was fueled by the knowledge that he was choosing more than a career path - he was choosing his destiny.

High school graduation was not just an end; it was a beginning. The stage was set for Duke to enter the realm of higher education, to join the ranks of aspiring engineers who shared his passion for innovation. The road ahead would be challenging, filled with late-night study sessions, complex equations, and moments of doubt. Yet, in the midst of it all, Duke held onto the spark of his dream, knowing that every challenge was a stepping stone toward the realization of his vision.

As the graduation ceremony approached and the halls of his high school echoed with nostalgia, Duke stood at the crossroads with a heart unyielding in its purpose. The future awaited him, and he was ready to seize it with both hands. The echoes of engines and the gleam of metal would guide his journey, propelling him toward the destiny he had always envisioned.

THE UNIVERSITY BOUND

The day of departure had dawned, a mixture of excitement and bittersweet farewells. Duke's childhood room, once a sanctuary for his dreams, now stood as a testament to his growth. Packed bags and memories lined the floor, a mosaic of the past and the future. With his parents standing by, Duke closed the door to his room one last time, ready to step onto the threshold of his next adventure.

As the car glided through familiar streets, Duke's gaze shifted from the scenery outside to the horizon ahead. The university campus, a sprawling landscape of possibilities, awaited his arrival. Anticipation pulsed through his veins, a current of energy that mirrored the hum of engines he so deeply admired.

The air was charged with the fervour of new beginnings as Duke set foot on campus. The atmosphere buzzed with the excitement of fresh faces, each carrying dreams and aspirations that painted the canvas of their future. The energy was palpable, a tapestry of ambitions interwoven with the promise of knowledge and growth.

Duke's heart raced as he navigated through the labyrinthine campus, finding his way to the engineering department. The lecture halls and laboratories that lay ahead held the keys to unlocking the mysteries of his passion. With each step, the weight of responsibility mingled with the exhilaration of possibility.

The first day of classes dawned, and Duke found himself in a lecture hall filled with fellow students, all eager to embark on this journey of discovery. The professor's words resonated with Duke, their significance echoing in his mind. Equations that once seemed abstract began to take on meaning, and concepts that had been foreign transformed into stepping stones toward his dreams.

In the laboratories, Duke's hands met engines, circuitry, and components that he had previously only seen in textbooks and diagrams. The tactile experience, the smell of grease and the hum of machinery, connected him to his passion in ways he had only imagined. With each experiment, he was one step closer to understanding the mechanics that fueled his dreams.

Yet, as the days turned into weeks and the weeks into months, Duke encountered challenges that tested his resolve. The late nights spent poring over equations and the frustration of projects that refused to yield to his efforts pushed him to his limits. Doubts crept in, the kind that whispered whether he was truly cut out for this path.

Amid the challenges, Duke found solace in the camaraderie of his peers. The friendships that blossomed in the lecture halls and labs became a lifeline, a reminder that he was not alone on this journey. Julia's quick wit, Abram's mechanical prowess, and the support of his friends breathed life into his determination.

Through the ups and downs, Duke held onto the driving force that had brought him here: his unyielding passion for cars and engineering. The late-night conversations with his father, the memories of car show, and the echo of his dreams in the lecture halls fortified his commitment. Each setback was a lesson, each triumph a step forward.

As the months turned into semesters, Duke's understanding deepened, and the pieces of the automotive puzzle began to fall into place. The university was not just a campus; it was a crucible where his passion was refined, his knowledge expanded, and his dreams stoked into an inferno of potential.

And so, Duke's university journey had begun. The stepping stones that he had meticulously placed were leading him toward a horizon that shimmered with promise. With each lecture attended, each lab conducted, and each challenge overcome, he was one step closer to understanding the mechanics that fueled his dreams.

BONDS OF FRIENDSHIP

Amid the whirlwind of lectures, labs, and a campus teeming with energy, Duke's path intersected with two individuals whose presence would shape his university experience in unexpected ways. Julia, with her computer science acumen, and Abram, a master of mechanics, became not just his classmates but kindred spirits bound by a shared passion for innovation.

Their friendship was a fusion of contrasts that created a harmonious synergy. Julia's tech-savviness, matched with Duke's automotive fervour and Abram's mechanical prowess, formed a trifecta of complementary skills. They were more than just friends; they were a team of dreamers, united by a common thread that transcended their individual pursuits.

As Duke tackled complex equations and delved into the intricacies of engineering, Julia was a constant presence by his side. Her wit and insight added layers of perspective to Duke's understanding, bridging the gap between the digital realm and the mechanics he was mastering.

Together, they explored how technology and engineering intertwined, each discovery sparking new avenues of curiosity. Abram, with his innate understanding of mechanics, brought a hands-on dimension to their trio.

His ability to dissect and rebuild machines was matched only by his boundless creativity. Whether it was brainstorming innovative solutions or transforming scraps into functional prototypes, Abram's practical approach added a tangible reality to Duke and Julia's ideas.

Their shared pursuit of knowledge was balanced by moments of respite, where they found laughter in the simplest things. Late-night study sessions evolved into light-hearted discussions about cars, technology, and dreams. The camaraderie that had blossomed within the confines of lecture halls expanded to include moments of bonding over shared meals, shared setbacks, and shared triumphs.

As the semesters unfolded, Duke, Julia, and Abram formed a nucleus of support for each other. Challenges that once seemed insurmountable were met with combined determination, and victories that were once solitary became communal celebrations. Through ups and downs, they fortified their connection, discovering that friendship was not just about shared interests, but about shared growth.

Their bond would soon be tested in ways they could never have foreseen. The storms that awaited them would challenge their unity, and the crucible of adversity would reveal the strength of their foundation. But for now, in the halls of academia and the corridors of discovery, Duke's friendship with Julia and Abram remained a beacon of inspiration, a testament to the power of shared passion and unwavering support.

THE SPARK OF LOVE

Within the tapestry of university life, as Duke navigated the complexities of lectures, labs, and friendships, an unexpected thread began to weave itself into his story. It was a thread of love, one that emerged from the most serendipitous of encounters and illuminated his life in ways he had never imagined.

Merriam was a fellow student whose presence radiated warmth and creativity. With a penchant for art and a smile that could brighten even the cloudiest day, she brought a vibrancy to the campus that was impossible to ignore. Her passion for creating, whether through sketches, paintings, or heartfelt conversations, was a magnetic force that drew Duke toward her.

Their paths converged during a campus event that celebrated the intersection of art and technology. It was an event Duke had attended out of curiosity, a desire to see how the worlds of engineering and creativity could merge. Little did he know that this event would mark the beginning of a new chapter in his life.

Amidst the crowd, their eyes met. It was a moment suspended in time; a connection forged by the universe itself. Merriam's laughter rang out like a melody, and her eyes sparkled with a curiosity that mirrored Duke's own. A conversation began, one that flowed effortlessly as they discovered shared interests and aspirations.

Velocity of Hope

In Merriam, Duke found someone who understood the depth of his passion. She saw beyond the equations and diagrams, embracing the essence of his dreams. Their discussions evolved into late-night conversations, where they shared their fears, ambitions, and the stories that had shaped them.

As the semesters passed, Duke's feelings for Merriam deepened, each interaction igniting a spark of connection that refused to fade. He admired her artistic soul and the way her creativity breathed life into every corner of her world. With her by his side, Duke discovered a new dimension to his own journey, one enriched by her presence and her unwavering belief in him.

Their love story was a tapestry woven with shared dreams and stolen glances across lecture halls. It was a dance of vulnerability, where two hearts dared to open themselves to each other. And as their connection blossomed, Duke realized that love was not a distraction from his dreams, but a source of inspiration that fueled his pursuit of engineering and innovation.

Amid the equations and experiments, Duke's heart found solace in the warmth of Merriam's smile. Their love story, born in the corridors of academia, was a reminder that life was a mosaic of experiences, and that the pursuit of passion could coexist with the pursuit of love. As Duke continued on his journey, he carried with him the spark that had kindled between them, a flame that illuminated not just his path, but the road ahead for both of them.

DREAMS UNVEILED

Duke's journey through the realm of engineering was a transformative odyssey, a symphony of mechanics, design, and innovation that would shape his destiny. As semesters rolled by, each one brought him closer to the heart of his dreams.

The lecture halls became temples of knowledge, where equations danced on chalkboards and concepts were dissected with precision. Duke's professors recognized his unwavering dedication, a fire that burned brightly in his eyes whenever he delved into the complexities of his field. Their encouragement fueled his determination, pushing him to explore the depths of mechanics and design with a thirst for understanding that knew no bounds.

Late nights in the laboratory became Duke's sanctuary. Amidst the hum of machines and the scent of oil, he immersed himself in projects that tested his skills and pushed the boundaries of his creativity. Whether it was designing the perfect gear ratio or crafting a prototype that defied conventional norms, every challenge was met with a fervour that only grew stronger with each obstacle.

Duke's efforts were not in vain. With the guidance of his professors and the support of his friends, including Julia and Abram, his understanding of engineering deepened. The mechanics that had once been enigmatic became familiar territory, and the world of design evolved into a canvas on which he could paint his visions.

Through sleepless nights and iterations that demanded both patience and persistence, Duke chiselled his dreams into something tangible. His designs were more than just blueprints; they were manifestations of his passion, reflections of the countless hours he had spent honing his craft. Each project became a step closer to his ultimate goal: to design and create a car that bore the mark of his ingenuity.

As the years went by, Duke's professors saw not only an exceptional student but a relentless dreamer. His dedication was a testament to his belief that the fusion of mechanics and design could birth innovation that transcended limits. The fire in his eyes told a story of resilience, of someone who had stared challenges in the face and emerged stronger, armed with knowledge and a relentless pursuit of excellence.

And so, within the walls of academia, Duke's dreams were unveiled. With each lecture absorbed, each equation solved, and each project completed, he was sculpting a path that led him closer to the realization of his vision. The journey had been arduous, but the road ahead glimmered with the promise of fulfillment. And as Duke's hands continued to meld his dreams, the world awaited the unveiling of his masterpiece.

TRAGEDY STRIKES

Amid the backdrop of Duke's pursuit of engineering excellence, a storm of tragedy brewed, shattering the tranquillity of his life. The night had started like any other, a casual outing with friends to unwind from the rigors of academia. But in a heartbeat, the course of Duke's journey would take a drastic and unforeseen turn.

In a crowded club, laughter and music filled the air as Duke and his friends, including Abram, Julia, and others, revelled in the freedom of the moment. Amidst the pulsating rhythm, an altercation erupted - a spark that ignited a chain reaction of events that would reverberate through their lives.

The altercation escalated beyond control, fueled by misunderstanding and the volatile mix of emotions. In the chaos, a gunshot shattered the night's veneer of celebration, and the world around Duke slowed to a surreal crawl. The unthinkable had happened - a dear friend, Jabu, lay lifeless on the floor, a victim of the violence that had erupted.

The shockwave of grief radiated through Duke and his friends, leaving them reeling and struggling to make sense of the nightmare that had unfolded. As they attempted to process the tragedy, their sorrow was entangled with confusion and a growing unease. The club had been a whirlwind of chaos, with accusations flying and the truth obscured by the fog of panic.

In the aftermath, fingers were pointed, suspicions cast, and Duke found himself in the eye of a storm he could never have predicted. Accusations swirled around him, fueled by the chaos of the night and the fog of uncertainty. The weight of suspicion bore down on his shoulders, and the innocence he had always carried now hung precariously in the balance.

With the wheels of justice set in motion, Duke's life was irrevocably altered. The camaraderie of friendship had been overshadowed by the darkness of tragedy, and he found himself grappling not only with grief but with the reality that he was being accused of a crime he did not commit. The courtroom, once a distant concept, now loomed on the horizon, a stark reminder that the threads of his life had been woven into a complex tapestry of events beyond his control.

As Duke navigated the storm of accusations and the shadow of a trial that lay ahead, he drew strength from the bonds he had formed. The support of Julia, Abram, and his friends became a lifeline as he faced the uncertainty that enveloped him. The journey of friendship that had once been a beacon of light was now a fortress against the storm, a reminder that he was not alone in his struggle.

Velocity of Hope

With his dreams of engineering excellence now intertwined with the nightmare of accusation, Duke's journey took an unforeseen detour. As he stepped into the uncharted territory of the legal system, his resilience would be tested in ways he could never have imagined. And as the trial loomed on the horizon, Duke's determination to prove his innocence burned brighter than ever, a fire that refused to be extinguished by the darkness that had descended upon his life.

DARK DAYS

In the wake of the tragic events that had unfolded in the club, Duke's life plunged into a dark abyss. The laughter and camaraderie that had once defined his days were replaced by the weight of uncertainty and the suffocating grip of accusations. The storm of tragedy had given way to the tempest of a legal battle, and Duke found himself ensnared in its relentless current.

Arrested and facing the gravest of accusations - murder - Duke's world was upended. The familiar halls of academia and the excitement of engineering had given way to cold, sterile rooms and the clinking of chains. The journey that had once seemed boundless had now come to a screeching halt, replaced by a reality that he could never have anticipated.

As the legal process unfolded, the darkness of Duke's days was magnified by the weight of the world around him. The walls of his cell seemed to close in, the isolation mirroring the confinement of his spirit. The accusatory stares of those who once knew him as a friend pierced through his resolve, and the tendrils of doubt that had taken root threatened to engulf him.

Velocity of Hope

Dreams of cars and innovation, once a fire that burned within him, now seemed distant and unattainable. The vision he had held for his future was eclipsed by the reality of his present - the uncertainty of the trial, the suffocating grip of suspicion, and the daunting possibility of a life forever altered.

In the midst of the darkness, Duke clung to the memories of better days - the laughter shared with friends, the discussions about engines that had once lit up his eyes, and the unwavering support of those who believed in his innocence. Julia, Abram, and his friends remained steadfast, a beacon of hope that pierced through the gloom.

As the days turned into nights and the nights into weeks, Duke's resolve was tested to its limits. Yet, even in the midst of despair, a spark of determination flickered within him. The fire that had fueled his dreams was not extinguished; it was merely dimmed by the circumstances he found himself in. And in the quiet moments of solitude, he held onto the belief that the truth would eventually emerge, dispelling the shadows that had cast doubt upon his character.

The dark days were a crucible that tested Duke's spirit and resilience. The weight of the world pressed down upon him, threatening to crush his dreams and define his destiny. But within that darkness, a glimmer of hope remained, a testament to the strength of his spirit and the power of friendship. As Duke navigated the treacherous waters of his legal battle, he carried within him the flicker of determination that had once ignited his dreams - a light that refused to be extinguished, even in the face of the darkest of days.

UNBREAKABLE BONDS

In the midst of Duke's darkest hours, when the storm of accusations and uncertainty raged around him, he found solace in the unwavering support of his closest friends. Julia, Abram, and Merriam stood by his side like pillars of strength, their belief in his innocence a lifeline that kept him anchored amidst the tempest.

The bond Duke had formed with Julia and Abram during their university days had transcended the boundaries of friendship. They were not just companions in good times; they were a fortress of solidarity when the world turned against him. Their shared history, the late-night conversations, and the camaraderie of pursuing dreams together had forged a connection that was unbreakable.

Julia's analytical mind and empathetic heart were a source of comfort for Duke. Her unyielding belief in his character and the meticulous research she conducted became a beacon of hope in the labyrinth of doubt. While the world accused, Julia stood by his side, reminding him that he was not alone in the battle for truth.

Abram, with his mechanical prowess and practical approach, lent Duke strength that transcended words. His steadfast presence, the unspoken understanding that flowed between them, was a testament to the bond they shared. With each visit and every reassuring smile, Abram reaffirmed the fact that, even in the face of adversity, Duke had a friend who would stand with him.

And then there was Merriam, the beacon of love and support that illuminated even the darkest corners of Duke's days. Their connection had deepened amidst the turmoil, a testament to the resilience of their hearts. Merriam's belief in Duke's character was unwavering, her presence a reminder that love could weather even the fiercest of storms.

Together, the four friends formed a unit that would be tested beyond imagination. As Duke's trial loomed on the horizon, their bond was the unshakable foundation upon which he stood. Their presence, their belief, and their dedication became his source of strength, allowing him to face the legal battle with courage and resilience.

Amidst the chaos, the accusations, and the uncertainty, Duke clung to the unbreakable bonds he had forged. Their friendship was a testament to the power of solidarity, a reminder that even in the darkest of times, there was a network of unwavering support that he could lean on.

As he faced the trial that would determine his fate, Duke knew that he was not alone. Julia, Abram, and Merriam were with him every step of the way, their unwavering belief in his innocence shining like a beacon of hope in the night.

A PARENT'S AGONY

News of Duke's arrest sent shockwaves through Joseph and Tina's world, shattering the veneer of success and stability they had worked so hard to build. The pillars that had supported their lives suddenly felt fragile, and they found themselves thrust into a vortex of emotions that they could never have prepared for.

Joseph and Tina, who had built their business from humble beginnings and witnessed Duke's growth into a determined young man, were now faced with a reality that defied their comprehension. The weight of the accusations against their son bore down on them, and their hearts were heavy with a mixture of disbelief, sorrow, and helplessness.

As parents, their agony was a torrential storm that raged within them. The news had peeled away the layers of their carefully curated life, leaving them raw and vulnerable. The questions echoed in their minds - How could this have happened? How could their son, whom they had watched grow into a dreamer with a heart full of ambition, be caught in such a nightmare?

Their days became a whirlwind of emotions as they grappled with the reality that their son's future hung in the balance. Their business, once a symbol of their triumph over adversity, now felt secondary to the battle that Duke was facing.

The camaraderie they had nurtured as a family was tested, and they found themselves torn between the desire to support their son and the weight of the allegations that threatened to tear their world apart.

Joseph's hands, once skilled in the art of mechanics, now trembled as he read news articles and legal documents that seemed to paint a damning picture. Tina's heart, which had once swelled with pride at Duke's accomplishments, now ached with a pain that defied description. Together, they weathered the storm of emotions, seeking solace in each other's presence as they grappled with the reality of Duke's situation.

As the legal battle unfolded, Joseph and Tina found themselves caught in a web of uncertainty. They were parents whose roles had shifted from guiding their son's aspirations to grappling with a crisis that had blindsided them. The courtroom, a place they had only seen in movies and TV shows, now held the fate of their beloved child.

Their agony was amplified by the inability to shield Duke from the storm that raged around him. The natural instinct to protect their son clashed with the reality that they were powerless to change the course of events. They had to stand on the side-lines, watching as the legal system took its course, their hearts torn between the love for their son and the weight of the truth they were desperate to uncover.

In the midst of the storm, Joseph and Tina clung to the memories of the son they knew - the dreamer with a passion for cars, the determined young man who had embarked on a journey of engineering excellence. Their agony was a testament to the depth of their love and the lengths they were willing to go to ensure justice for Duke. As they faced the uncertainty that lay ahead, their bond as a family would be tested, their resolve pushed to its limits.

THE LEGAL BATTLE

Duke's life hung in the balance as the legal battle unfolded, a high-stakes confrontation that would decide whether he would emerge as a survivor or a scapegoat. The courtroom became an arena of justice, where truth and deception clashed in a struggle for clarity. Duke's Défense attorney became his shield, fighting tirelessly to unravel the layers of the case and unveil the reality behind that fateful night.

In the courtroom, Duke's Défense attorney, a beacon of determination, became his voice in the face of adversity. With each word spoken and every piece of evidence presented, they aimed to paint a portrait of Duke that defied the accusations that had been hurled against him. The attorney's strategy was clear - to peel back the layers of the night's events, exposing the intricate web of truth and lies that had woven together to form a tragic tableau.

As the trial progressed, the courtroom became a theatre of emotions. Witnesses took the stand, their testimonies revealing fragments of the puzzle that had led to Jabu's death. The prosecution sought to build a narrative that painted Duke as the aggressor, a portrayal that his attorney fought vehemently to dismantle. With every cross-examination, every question posed, the layers of doubt were chipped away, and the attorney's pursuit of truth remained unyielding.

Duke's attorney meticulously pieced together an alternative version of events, one that shone a light on the ambiguity and confusion of that night. They presented evidence that pointed to the presence of other individuals whose actions may have contributed to the tragedy. Fingerprints, timelines, and alibis were scrutinized, revealing inconsistencies that cast doubt on the initial accusations.

The trial was an emotional rollercoaster, as the weight of Duke's fate rested on the shoulders of those in the courtroom. Joseph and Tina, sitting in the gallery, held their breath with each new revelation, their hearts torn between hope and fear. Duke himself sat at the centre of it all, his determination to prove his innocence matched only by the desire to honour the memory of his friend who had been lost.

In the midst of the legal battle, the truth emerged like a phoenix rising from the ashes. A breakthrough came in the form of new evidence - fingerprints that belonged to a previously unknown individual, a gangster named Andrews. The discovery sent shockwaves through the courtroom, casting a new light on the events that had transpired that fateful night.

Duke's Défense attorney seized upon this revelation, presenting it as a game-changing piece of the puzzle. The narrative shifted, and the accusatory gaze turned toward a new direction. The attorney painted a picture of Duke as a victim of circumstance, caught in a web of events beyond his control.

Velocity of Hope

As the legal battle reached its crescendo, the courtroom braced for the verdict that would decide Duke's fate. The Défense attorney's tireless efforts, coupled with the emergence of new evidence, had cast doubt on the accusations that had once seemed irrefutable. As the jury deliberated, the tension was palpable, and Duke's future hung in the balance.

The legal battle was a crucible that tested Duke's resilience, his family's determination, and the power of truth to prevail over deception. Amidst the struggle for justice, the truth behind that tragic night would be unveiled, reshaping the narrative and revealing the complexities that had led to a life lost and a young man's future hanging in the balance.

UNVEILING TRUTHS

As the legal battle unfolded and the intricate web of events surrounding that tragic night was dissected in the courtroom, a glimmer of doubt began to emerge about Duke's guilt. The puzzle pieces that had once seemed to fit together so neatly now revealed gaps, inconsistencies that cast shadows over the accusations that had been hurled against him. Amidst the chaos of uncertainty, a new investigator entered the scene, armed with modern technology and a fresh perspective.

The courtroom became a theatre of revelations as evidence was presented, each piece of the puzzle contributing to a larger narrative that painted a different picture than what had initially been assumed. Witnesses were cross-examined, timelines were re-examined, and the details of that fateful night were scrutinized with a fine-tooth comb.

Duke's Défense attorney, relentless in their pursuit of truth, pieced together a new version of events that challenged the prevailing narrative. The emergence of new evidence, fingerprints belonging to a gangster named Andrews, was a turning point that sent shockwaves through the proceedings. The doubt that had taken root began to grow, and the walls of certainty crumbled.

Velocity of Hope

In the midst of this turmoil, a new investigator stepped onto the scene, armed with modern technology and a fresh perspective. Their arrival marked a turning point, as they leveraged advancements in forensics and digital analysis to re-examine the evidence that had been collected. With an analytical eye and a determination to uncover the truth, the investigator sought to shed light on the intricacies that had been missed in the initial chaos of the investigation.

Through the use of cutting-edge technology, the investigator peeled back layers of deception, revealing a more nuanced reality that had been obscured by assumptions and biases. Digital footprints were followed, connections were established, and a clearer understanding of the events leading up to the tragedy began to emerge.

As the courtroom held its collective breath, the investigator's findings were presented, shedding light on the presence of Andrews and his role in the events that had transpired.

The new insights provided a counter-narrative that raised questions about the accuracy of the initial accusations against Duke. The uncertainty that had clouded his innocence began to lift, and a sense of hope pervaded the proceedings.

The emergence of this new perspective was a turning point that sparked a renewed determination to uncover the truth. Doubts that had once been dismissed gained traction, and the lines between truth and deception blurred as the complexities of the situation were Unraveled. Duke's Défense attorney seized upon these revelations, weaving them into a narrative that challenged the assumptions that had led to his arrest.

As the courtroom proceedings continued, the investigator's role became pivotal, their efforts shining a light on the shadows of doubt and reshaping the landscape of truth. With technology as their ally, they peeled back the layers of deception that had obscured the reality of that tragic night.

Amidst the chaos of accusations and uncertainty, the pursuit of justice was propelled forward by the revelations that emerged, igniting a beacon of hope in the quest to unveil the truths that had long been concealed.

THE INVESTIGATOR'S REVELATION

As the new investigator delved into the intricate web of events that had led to the tragedy, their findings cast a new light on the situation. Fingerprint evidence, surveillance footage, and witness testimonies began to converge, painting a more complex and nuanced narrative than had initially been assumed. Duke's name wasn't yet cleared, but the shadow of doubt was growing, shrouding the accusations that had once seemed ironclad.

The courtroom became a stage upon which the investigator's revelations unfolded, each piece of evidence presented like a puzzle piece that contributed to the larger picture. Fingerprint analysis revealed a pattern that led to Andrews, the gangster whose presence had been discovered at the scene. Surveillance footage, once a blur of chaotic movement, was now dissected frame by frame, uncovering moments that had previously been overlooked.

The investigator's findings provided a counterpoint to the prosecution's narrative, and as they presented their discoveries, a sense of tension filled the air. The precision with which they connected the dots, revealing a chain of events that had led to the tragedy, was both captivating and unsettling. Witness testimonies were re-examined, inconsistencies highlighted, and the pieces of the puzzle began to fit together in unexpected ways.

Duke's Défense attorney seized upon the investigator's revelations, weaving them into a narrative that countered the accusations that had once seemed insurmountable. The shadow of doubt that now loomed over the case was a testament to the power of the truth to unravel even the most tightly woven web of assumptions.

As the trial continued, the emergence of this new perspective was a turning point that shifted the trajectory of Duke's fate. The complexity of the narrative was a reminder that life's events were rarely black and white, and that the pursuit of justice demanded a relentless commitment to uncovering every facet of the truth.

Joseph and Tina, who had clung to hope amidst the storm, found their faith bolstered by the investigator's revelations. The shadow of doubt provided a glimmer of optimism, a ray of light that pierced through the clouds of uncertainty. Their agony, born from a parent's love for their child, began to give way to a cautious optimism that justice might prevail.

In the midst of the investigator's revelation, the narrative of that tragic night began to shift. The convergence of evidence, the unraveling of assumptions, and the emergence of a more complex truth painted a different picture than had initially been assumed.

The courtroom, once a place of certainty, was now a battleground of competing perspectives, each fighting for dominance in the quest for truth.

As the investigator's findings echoed in the hearts of those present, the uncertainty of Duke's fate was both daunting and hopeful. The narrative of that night was being rewritten, and amidst the chaos of accusations and doubt, the pursuit of justice marched forward, led by the revelations that had reshaped the landscape of truth.

THE TURN OF TIDES

The courtroom hummed with an electric anticipation as the trial reached a pivotal juncture. The air was thick with tension, each heartbeat echoing the gravity of the moment. All eyes were on the defence as they stepped forward to present their case, armed with evidence that had the potential to challenge the very foundation of the accusations against Duke.

Duke's defence attorney, fueled by determination and armed with the investigator's revelations, weaved together the threads of evidence with a deftness that demanded attention. Their words were a symphony of logic and emotion, a tapestry that challenged the initial assumptions that had once seemed unassailable. With each piece of evidence presented, a new perspective began to emerge, and the jury's collective gaze shifted, no longer bound by the confines of the story they had been told.

Witness testimonies were re-examined, alibis questioned, and timelines dissected. The intricate puzzle of that ill-fated night was reconstructed in a way that cast doubt upon the prevailing narrative. The defence attorney's voice echoed in the hushed courtroom, a voice that sought to unravel the complexities and reveal a truth that had long been obscured.

Velocity of Hope

The convergence of evidence pointed to a more nuanced reality, one that challenged the binary notion of guilt and innocence. Fingerprint analysis, surveillance footage, and witness statements formed a mosaic that painted a different picture of the events leading up to the tragedy. The defence's argument was not that Duke was innocent, but that the truth was far more intricate than had initially been assumed.

As the defence presented its case, the atmosphere in the courtroom shifted. Doubt began to creep in, undermining the confidence that had once held the prosecution's narrative together. The jury, once swayed by certainty, now found themselves grappling with the shades of grey that the defence had introduced. The story they thought they knew was being deconstructed, reshaped by the revelation of new perspectives and insights.

Joseph and Tina, seated in the gallery, held their breath as they watched the courtroom drama unfold. The turn of tides was a glimmer of hope that their son's innocence might be recognized, a culmination of the agonizing journey they had embarked upon since that fateful night. Their hearts swayed with each word spoken by the defence, their hopes and fears entwined in the outcome that loomed on the horizon.

In the midst of the courtroom drama, the narrative of that night shifted. The threads of evidence, once woven into a seamless tapestry of accusation, were now being Unraveled, revealing a more complex truth. The jurors' eyes, once fixed on the prosecution's version of events, began to shift, their thoughts carried away by the tide of uncertainty that the defence had introduced.

As the trial moved forward, the turn of tides became a beacon of change in the pursuit of justice. The narrative was no longer static; it was fluid, evolving with each revelation, each piece of evidence that was presented. The courtroom, once a battleground of certainty, had become a landscape of shifting perspectives, where the pursuit of truth demanded an unwavering commitment to uncovering the layers of complexity that had long been obscured.

THE WEIGHT OF ACQUITTAL

After a trial that had been marked by twists and revelations, the moment of truth finally arrived. The courtroom held its collective breath, the air charged with tension and anticipation. Emotions ran high as the jury delivered its verdict, and the weight of the accusations that had hung over Duke for so long was finally lifted.

The courtroom, once a stage for accusations and counterarguments, was now a theatre of high-stakes resolution. The faces of those present mirrored the intensity of the moment, each heartbeat resonating with the gravity of what was to come. Joseph and Tina, seated in the gallery, clung to each other's hands, their eyes fixed on the jury as they prepared to deliver the verdict that would shape their son's future.

The silence in the room was palpable as the jury's decision was read aloud. The word "acquittal" hung in the air like a melody, a testament to the power of the truth to prevail over deception. Duke, who had faced the storm of accusations with unwavering determination, stood at the centre of it all, his heart pounding with a mixture of hope and anxiety.

As the weight of the accusations was lifted, a collective exhale seemed to sweep through the room. Tears welled in the eyes of Duke's supporters, and a mixture of relief and disbelief washed over them. The truth, like a stubborn seed, had pushed its way through the soil of doubt, breaking free from the constraints that had sought to smother it.

Duke's attorney, the defender of truth in the face of adversity, smiled as they exchanged glances with their client. Their tireless efforts, the countless hours of research and argumentation, had culminated in a moment of triumph. The weight of the acquittal was a validation of their dedication, a testament to their unwavering commitment to justice.

For Joseph and Tina, the moment was an emotional culmination of a journey that had tested their resilience as parents. The agony they had endured, the sleepless nights and the anguished prayers, were now transformed into tears of relief and joy. The weight that had pressed down upon their hearts for so long had been lifted, replaced by a sense of renewal and hope for the future.

Duke himself stood as a symbol of resilience and the power of truth. The accusations that had threatened to define his life were now relegated to the past, replaced by the promise of a new beginning. As he looked around the courtroom, his eyes met those of his friends - Julia, Abram, and Merriam - who had stood by his side through the darkest of days.

The weight of acquittal was more than a legal verdict; it was a testament to the strength of the human spirit and the unwavering pursuit of justice. As the courtroom emptied and the reality of his newfound freedom settled in, Duke felt the weight of the accusations lift, replaced by the knowledge that the truth had prevailed, and that he could now embrace the future with a renewed sense of purpose and determination.

HEALING WOUNDS

With the trial finally concluded and the weight of accusations lifted, Duke found himself standing at a crossroads. The wounds, both visible and hidden, were a reminder of the ordeal he had endured. But as he looked ahead, he was determined to embark on a journey of healing, a path that would lead him towards rebuilding his life and reclaiming his dreams.

The scars left by the trial were not just physical; they were etched into Duke's psyche. The uncertainty, the accusations, and the long road to exoneration had left their mark, a reminder of the resilience it had taken to weather the storm. The journey of healing was not one that could be rushed, but Duke was determined to take each step with purpose and strength.

Amidst the healing process, Merriam's presence became a soothing balm to Duke's wounded heart. Her unwavering support, the love that had persisted even in the darkest of times, was a source of comfort that he could lean on. Their connection had deepened through the trials they had faced together, and the bond they shared was a testament to the strength of their love.

Velocity of Hope

As Duke navigated the path of healing, he found solace in returning to his passion for cars. The dreams that had driven him before the trial still burned within him, and he channelled his energy into his engineering studies with renewed determination. The scars, instead of holding him back, became a reminder of his resilience and the hurdles he had overcome.

Merriam's presence was a constant reminder that healing was not a solitary journey. Her support was an anchor that steadied him as he confronted the memories and emotions that had been stirred by the trial. With each day that passed, Duke found himself gaining strength, the wounds of the past gradually giving way to the promise of a brighter future.

In the midst of his own healing, Duke also witnessed the resilience of his parents, Joseph and Tina. Their journey had been one of anguish and hope, and as they navigated the aftermath of the trial, they showed a steadfast commitment to supporting their son. Their love and strength were a source of inspiration, a reminder that family bonds could weather even the fiercest of storms.

As Duke's wounds slowly began to heal, he realized that the scars were not a mark of weakness, but a testament to his strength. The journey he had embarked upon had tested his character and pushed him to his limits, but he had emerged on the other side with a renewed sense of purpose. With Merriam by his side, he felt a growing sense of hope, a belief that the future held the promise of fulfillment and the realization of his dreams.

The healing journey was not without its challenges, but Duke faced them with the same determination that had carried him through the trial. As he looked ahead, he knew that the scars of the past were a part of his story, a reminder of the battles he had fought and the resilience he had discovered within himself. And as he continued to heal, he found himself embracing the future with a newfound sense of strength and optimism.

NAVIGATING RELATIONSHIPS

The trials and tribulations of the past had not only left their mark on Duke, but had also reshaped the landscape of his relationships with his friends. The bonds that had once felt unbreakable had been tested by the storm they had weathered together, and as they sought to mend the frayed threads of their connection; new dynamics began to emerge.

The experience had altered them, leaving each of Duke's friends with their own scars and vulnerabilities. The camaraderie that had once been so effortless now required effort and understanding. Julia, Abram, and Merriam had all stood by Duke's side through the trial, and in doing so, had also confronted their own emotions and fears.

The process of navigating these altered relationships was both delicate and transformative. Secrets were shared, walls were lowered, and vulnerabilities were exposed. The veil of invincibility that had once shrouded their friendships was now replaced with a deeper sense of intimacy. The conversations they had were no longer surface-level; they delved into the depths of their emotions, addressing the wounds that had been inflicted by the events of the past.

For Julia, the experience had highlighted the fragility of life and the importance of cherishing every moment. As a computer science major, her analytical mind found solace in unraveling the intricacies of the situation. Through their conversations, she discovered a newfound sense of empathy, understanding the weight of Duke's journey and the strength it had taken to endure.

Abram, the mechanical whiz, had always been a pillar of support for Duke. But the trial had revealed his own struggles with fear and doubt. The near-loss of his friend had forced him to confront his vulnerabilities and recognize that strength wasn't solely defined by physical prowess. The experience had humbled him and deepened his connection with Duke and the others.

Merriam, whose unwavering presence had been Duke's anchor, had faced her own emotional turmoil. The fear of losing the person she loved most had been a constant companion, and as they navigated their shared healing journey, they discovered a new level of intimacy. Their bond, once built on the foundation of friendship, had transformed into a love that was fortified by the challenges they had faced together.

Through their shared vulnerability and openness, the ties that bound Duke and his friends grew stronger. The wounds of the past were acknowledged, and in their place, a sense of mutual understanding and support emerged. The trials they had faced together had shattered the illusion of invulnerability, but in its wake, they discovered a deeper, more meaningful connection.

As they navigated these new dynamics, Duke realized that the journey of healing wasn't a solitary one. The threads of friendship that had been frayed by adversity were now being rewoven, creating a tapestry that was richer and more intricate than before. Their relationships were no longer defined solely by shared interests and good times; they were also shaped by the challenges they had overcome and the growth they had experienced.

In the midst of it all, Duke's relationships with Julia, Abram, and Merriam became a source of strength and inspiration. The transformation they had undergone was a testament to the resilience of the human spirit and the power of enduring connections. As they continued to navigate the complexities of their friendships, they found themselves embracing the truth that adversity could not only reveal vulnerabilities, but also forge bonds that were unbreakable.

A LONG ROAD TO RECOVERY

Duke's return to university marked a significant step in his journey of recovery. The campus that had once been a place of hope and opportunity now held the echoes of the trial that had turned his life upside down. As he stepped back onto familiar grounds, he carried with him a mix of relief and anxiety, a complex blend of emotions that reflected the long road he had travelled.

The weight of the past still lingered, casting a shadow over his aspirations. The scars of the trial were not easily forgotten, and Duke found himself grappling with a range of emotions - from moments of triumph to lingering doubts. The stares of curiosity and the whispers that followed in his wake served as constant reminders of the ordeal he had endured.

Despite the challenges, Duke was determined to face his studies with renewed vigor. The dream of becoming an engineer, of designing his own brand of car, burned within him as brightly as ever. With each step he took towards his classes, he carried with him the lessons he had learned through adversity - the importance of resilience, the value of determination, and the power of community.

Julia, Abram, and Merriam continued to stand by his side, their unwavering support serving as a source of strength. They navigated the campus together, facing the curious glances and questions with a united front. Their presence was a reminder that Duke was not alone in his journey, that the trials they had faced had forged a bond that transcended the challenges they had overcome.

The university itself became a place of renewal, a canvas upon which Duke could paint his future. The pursuit of engineering, once a distant dream, was now a reality that he could grasp. His studies became a sanctuary, a space where he could channel his energy and determination. The complexity of the coursework mirrored the complexities of his own life, and each challenge he overcame served as a testament to his resilience.

As the days turned into weeks and the weeks into semesters, Duke's progress was a testament to his unwavering commitment to recovery. The weight of the past slowly began to lift as he immersed himself in his studies and his friendships. He engaged in conversations about engineering and design with a passion that was undiminished by the trials he had faced.

With each achievement, no matter how small, Duke found himself regaining the confidence that had been shaken by the trial. The dream of designing his own brand of car remained a beacon on the horizon, a goal that fueled his determination to overcome the obstacles in his path. And with the support of his friends and the newfound resilience he had discovered within himself, he was prepared to travel the long road to recovery with a spirit that was unyielding.

As Duke faced his studies with renewed vigor, he realized that the journey of recovery was not linear, nor was it without its challenges. But with each step he took, he found himself moving forward, closer to a future that was defined not by the trials he had faced, but by the determination and strength he had discovered within himself.

THE UNSEEN HERO

Amidst the tumultuous proceedings of the trial, one figure had remained in the shadows, overlooked amidst the chaos and accusations - Andrews, the enigmatic gangster whose actions had set off the tragic chain of events. As the truth began to slowly unravel, the story of Andrews' role in the ordeal emerged, revealing a complex narrative that went beyond the surface of his actions.

For much of the trial, Andrews had been painted as a shadowy figure, a villain lurking on the periphery of the tragedy. His presence had cast a dark cloud over the events of that ill-fated night, with accusations and suspicions pointing towards his involvement. Yet, as the layers of the story were peeled back, a more nuanced portrait of Andrews began to emerge.

The truth, like a mosaic assembled piece by piece, revealed that Andrews was not the mastermind many had believed him to be. He was not the puppeteer pulling the strings, but rather a pawn in a much larger game that had spiralled out of control. As the details of his involvement were uncovered, a different perspective on his actions began to take shape.

Andrews had been caught in a web of circumstances that went beyond his control. The gangster life he had been living was not one of his own choosing, but rather a product of the environment he had grown up in. His motivations were complex and intertwined with forces that extended far beyond the events of that fateful night.

As the trial progressed and the evidence was presented, the role of external pressures and influences became apparent. Andrews had been manipulated and coerced, forced into a situation that had catastrophic consequences. His actions had been a reflection of the limited choices available to him, rather than a manifestation of pure malevolence.

The revelation of Andrews' true role in the tragedy was a reminder of the complexity of human behaviour and the power of external factors to shape one's actions. The courtroom, once a place of judgment, now became a forum for understanding the layers of truth that had been concealed beneath the surface. Andrews' story served as a cautionary tale, highlighting the far-reaching impact of circumstances beyond an individual's control.

In the wake of these revelations, the lines between victim and perpetrator began to blur. Andrews was not absolved of responsibility, but rather his actions were contextualized within the broader narrative of the events that had transpired. The unseen hero of this chapter was the truth itself, a force that illuminated the hidden corners of the story and reshaped the perceptions that had been formed in the shadows of ignorance.

As the trial continued to unfold, the complex tale of Andrews' involvement added another layer of depth to the narrative. The unseen hero of the story was not a singular figure, but rather the pursuit of truth and understanding, shedding light on the complexities of human behaviour and the intricate interplay of circumstances that could lead even the most unlikely of figures down a path they could never have foreseen.

REBUILDING DREAMS

With the weight of accusations finally lifted and his innocence established, Duke found himself standing at the threshold of a new chapter in his life. The trial, with all its trials and tribulations, had cleared the path for him to pursue the very dream that had fueled his aspirations since childhood. With a renewed sense of clarity and purpose, he embarked on the journey of rebuilding his dreams.

As he stepped back into the halls of the university, a sense of determination surged within him. The engineering studies that had once felt like an insurmountable challenge were now a canvas upon which he could paint his future. Duke's return to his studies was marked not only by a desire to excel, but also by a profound appreciation for the opportunity to do so.

The sketches that had adorned his childhood room took on a new significance. What had once been mere drawings now held the promise of becoming tangible creations. Those sketches were the blueprints of his future, the visual manifestations of the dreams that had carried him through the storm. Each line and curve represented a piece of the puzzle that was slowly coming together.

Velocity of Hope

With a newfound sense of purpose, Duke immersed himself in his studies. The trials and challenges of the past had shaped him into a more focused and resilient individual. The intricate mechanics, the complexities of design, and the principles of engineering were no longer daunting; they were exciting puzzles waiting to be solved.

Julia, Abram, and Merriam continued to stand by his side, celebrating each victory and offering support during moments of doubt. Their presence was a reminder that Duke was not walking this path alone. They had been witnesses to his journey, and their shared experiences had only deepened their bonds.

The dream of designing his own brand of car remained as vibrant as ever. Duke's sketches evolved into detailed plans, and his passion was evident in every line he drew. The setbacks and challenges he had faced had not deterred him; if anything, they had ignited a fire within him to prove that dreams were worth fighting for.

The university, once a place of uncertainty, now became a hub of inspiration and learning. The knowledge he gained, the friendships he nurtured, and the challenges he overcame were all stepping stones on his path to fulfillment. Duke's story was a testament to the power of resilience, the importance of never giving up on one's aspirations, and the capacity of the human spirit to overcome adversity.

As Duke continued to rebuild his dreams, he recognized that the journey was ongoing. The scars of the past were a reminder of the battles he had fought, but they were also symbols of his strength and determination. Each step he took, each line he sketched, brought him closer to the realization of his dream - a dream that had survived the trials of the past and emerged stronger, more vibrant, and more real than ever before.

A PARENT'S TRIUMPH

Joseph and Tina had stood as pillars of strength throughout the tumultuous journey that had unfolded. Their unwavering support for Duke was a testament to the depth of their love as parents, and as the trial concluded and their son emerged from the shadows of accusation, their journey was marked by a profound sense of triumph.

The challenges they had faced mirrored those of their son. The weight of accusations had taken a toll on their hearts, the agony of not being able to protect their child from the storm leaving scars that were not visible to the eye. But as they witnessed Duke's resilience, their own determination was fortified.

Their journey was one of setbacks and resilience, marked by sleepless nights and tearful prayers. Joseph's business acumen had prepared him to navigate challenges, but nothing could have prepared him for the emotional trial that his family endured. Tina's unwavering faith and love had been a constant source of strength, her presence serving as a reminder that they were not alone in their struggle.

As the trial progressed and the truth came to light, Joseph and Tina's emotions were a mixture of relief, joy, and a sense of vindication. The trial's conclusion was not just a victory for Duke; it was a triumph for the entire family. The legacy they had strived to build, the values they had instilled in their son, were reflected in the resilience he had shown in the face of adversity.

The courtroom proceedings had been a rollercoaster of emotions for Joseph and Tina. They had witnessed their son's character and integrity put to the test, and the accusations had felt like a personal attack on their family. Yet, as they sat in the gallery, watching the trial unfold, they drew strength from the same well of determination that Duke had tapped into.

As Duke's name was cleared and the truth prevailed, Joseph and Tina felt a sense of triumph that went beyond exoneration. They saw in their son the embodiment of their own values - the importance of resilience, the power of family bonds, and the capacity to rise above challenges. The scars they carried from the trial were now transformed into badges of honour, symbols of the battles they had fought together.

Duke's emergence from the shadows of accusation was not just his victory; it was a victory for the family as a whole. Joseph and Tina's journey had mirrored his, marked by darkness and light, pain and triumph. As they looked at their son, standing tall and unbroken, they saw the legacy they had strived to create - a legacy of strength, love, and unwavering support.

In the aftermath of the trial, Joseph and Tina continued to stand by Duke's side, celebrating his triumphs and offering guidance during moments of uncertainty. Their bond as a family had been tested, but it had emerged stronger than ever. Their story was a testament to the power of parental love, the strength of familial bonds, and the triumph that could be found in the face of adversity.

As they looked towards the future, Joseph and Tina knew that their journey was far from over. The scars of the past were a reminder of the battles they had fought, but they were also a reminder of the strength that had carried them through. Their triumph was not just in the conclusion of the trial, but in the legacy, they had built and the indomitable spirit they had instilled in their son - a spirit that would continue to guide him as he pursued his dreams and embraced the future with unwavering determination

THE BIRTH OF "DUKE"

As Duke's journey in engineering continued, his knowledge deepened, and with it, his vision for his car evolved into something even more profound. The trial had shaped him into a stronger individual, and as he walked the path of recovery, his determination to bring his dream to life burned brighter than ever before. With the unwavering support of his father's company, he embarked on the remarkable journey of designing the car that would come to be known as "Duke."

The process was more than just engineering; it was an artistic expression of his passion and his resilience. The sketches that had once adorned his room had transformed into detailed blueprints, capturing the intricate mechanics and the aesthetic beauty of the car. Each line he drew, each calculation he made, was a reflection of his dreams and the engineering prowess he had honed through adversity.

"Duke" was not merely a car; it was a symphony of precision and innovation, a testament to the power of dreams translated into reality. The design incorporated elements that Duke had admired in the cars that had fueled his passion since childhood. The sleek curves, the aerodynamic lines, and the blend of aesthetics and functionality came together in a harmonious fusion.

The journey of designing "Duke" was not without its challenges. Duke's engineering studies had provided him with the foundation, but turning his vision into reality required a deep dive into the intricacies of design, mechanics, and manufacturing. The days were long, the challenges were daunting, but Duke's determination never wavered. His commitment to his dream, coupled with the guidance of experienced mentors within his father's company, propelled him forward.

With each step he took in the design process, Duke's connection to the car deepened. It was more than just a project; it was a labour of love that carried the weight of his journey. The scars of the trial were a constant reminder of the resilience he had discovered within himself, and those scars were mirrored in the car's design - a reflection of the challenges faced and the triumphs achieved.

As the design of "Duke" took shape, so did the anticipation within Duke's heart. The car represented not only his passion for engineering, but also his victory over adversity. It was a symbol of his unyielding determination to turn dreams into reality, a testament to the unwavering support of his friends, family, and mentors.

The completion of the design marked a milestone in Duke's journey. The blueprint that had once existed only in his imagination was now a tangible reality, waiting to be crafted from metal and machinery. The trials he had faced had not just shaped his character; they had also shaped his creation, infusing it with a depth of meaning that transcended the physical form.

As Duke looked at the completed design of "Duke," he knew that the journey was far from over. The challenges of manufacturing, testing, and refining lay ahead. But just as he had navigated the trials of the past with unwavering determination, he was prepared to navigate the challenges of the future with the same spirit. The birth of "Duke" was not just the culmination of a dream; it was the beginning of a new chapter in Duke's life, a chapter filled with the promise of innovation, resilience, and the fulfillment of aspirations that had been kindled in the fires of adversity.

STRUGGLES OF SUCCESS

The journey of turning the dream of the "Duke" car into a reality was a testament to Duke's determination and resilience, but it was not without its share of challenges. As he delved into the process of bringing his vision to life, he encountered setbacks and design dilemmas that tested his dedication and resolve.

The transition from blueprint to reality was a complex endeavour. The intricacies of manufacturing, the precision required in the assembly process, and the fine-tuning of every component presented a new set of challenges. Duke's dedication was put to the test as he faced design dilemmas that seemed to defy resolution. The road to success was marked by moments of frustration and doubt, moments that questioned whether the dream he had nurtured for so long was truly attainable.

Amid the struggles, Duke found solace in the unwavering support of his friends - Julia, Abram, and Merriam. Their presence was a constant reminder that he was not alone in this endeavour. They offered a listening ear, a shoulder to lean on, and words of encouragement that carried him through moments of uncertainty. Their belief in him and his dream was a beacon of light in the midst of challenges.

Julia, with her analytical mind, provided a fresh perspective on the design dilemmas that Duke faced. Her insights often shed new light on possible solutions, and her unwavering belief in his abilities was a source of inspiration. Abram, whose mechanical expertise had always been a pillar of support, was there to troubleshoot and problem-solve, ensuring that every mechanical challenge was met with determination rather than defeat.

Merriam, with her artistic sensibility, reminded Duke that even the most beautiful symphonies had their off-notes. Her ability to see the beauty in imperfections served as a reminder that the journey to success was not a straight line, but a series of peaks and valleys that ultimately formed a unique and beautiful composition.

The struggles of success served as a crucible that tested Duke's commitment to his dream. Each setback was a reminder that the path to innovation was often paved with challenges, but it was in those challenges that growth and learning flourished. The frustrations he encountered were not signs of failure, but rather opportunities to refine and improve his design.

As Duke wrestled with the complexities of bringing "Duke" to life, he drew strength from the support of his friends and the lessons he had learned from his past trials. The scars of the trial were a testament to his ability to overcome adversity, and they served as a reminder that challenges could be conquered with determination and resilience.

Velocity of Hope

With each hurdle he cleared, Duke's determination burned even brighter. The setbacks he faced were not roadblocks, but stepping stones on his path to success. The struggles were not a sign of defeat, but rather a testament to his commitment to realizing his dreams.

As the process continued, Duke knew that the road ahead would not be easy, but he was prepared to face it with the same spirit that had carried him through the trials of the past. The "Duke" car was not just a vehicle; it was a manifestation of his journey, a symbol of the resilience, friendship, and unwavering belief that had carried him through the struggles of success.

THE MOTTO

As Duke's design for the "Duke" car neared completion, he faced a challenge that went beyond the realm of engineering. It was a challenge that required him to encapsulate the very essence of his creation, to distil its significance into a few words that would resonate with meaning and purpose. This challenge was not about mechanics; it was about capturing the heart and soul of his journey.

For days, Duke grappled with the task of finding a motto that would serve as the heartbeat of his creation. The "Duke" car was more than just a vehicle; it was a symbol of his resilience, a testament to his ability to overcome adversity, and a tribute to the unwavering support of his friends and family. The motto had to reflect all of this and more - it had to be a beacon of inspiration for those who would see, drive, and experience the car.

Duke's journey had been marked by trials, but it had also been characterized by his unyielding determination to rise above challenges. It was a journey that had taken him from the depths of despair to the pinnacle of triumph. And as he contemplated the words that would define his creation, he found himself drawn to a phrase that had deep personal meaning - "No weapons formed against you."

Velocity of Hope

This phrase, drawn from a wellspring of personal experiences, carried layers of significance. It was a declaration of triumph over adversity, a reminder that despite the challenges he had faced, Duke had emerged victorious. The words spoke to the power of resilience, the strength of the human spirit, and the capacity to overcome even the most daunting of obstacles.

The motto was more than just a phrase; it was a rallying cry, an anthem that encapsulated the essence of Duke's journey. It spoke to the trials he had faced, the doubts he had conquered, and the dreams he had pursued with unrelenting fervour. It was a testament to his unbreakable spirit and a promise that no matter the challenges that lay ahead, he would continue to persevere.

The process of arriving at this motto was not a solitary one. Duke engaged in discussions with his friends - Julia, Abram, and Merriam - seeking their insights and perspectives. Their input added depth and richness to the words he was crafting, ensuring that the motto resonated with the collective experiences they had shared.

As the words "No weapons formed against you" were etched onto the blueprint of the "Duke" car, they became more than just letters; they became a mantra that would guide Duke's journey into the future. The motto held the power to inspire those who would come into contact with the car, to remind them that challenges could be overcome and dreams could be realized.

With the motto in place, the "Duke" car was no longer just a creation of mechanics and design; it was a symbol of resilience, a celebration of triumph, and a declaration of Duke's unwavering determination. It was a fitting tribute to the journey he had undertaken, a journey that had transformed not only his dream, but also his very being. And as he looked at those words, Duke knew that they held the power to inspire not just himself, but all those who would encounter the car and the story it represented.

UNVEILING THE DREAM

The day that Duke had long dreamed of had finally arrived - the day when the "Duke" car would be unveiled to the world. The venue was alive with a palpable excitement, as industry insiders, media representatives, and car enthusiasts from all walks of life gathered to witness the culmination of Duke's vision. The air was electric with anticipation, and the atmosphere was charged with the energy of a dream about to be unveiled.

As the event unfolded, Duke's heart beat with a mixture of nervousness and determination. The journey that had begun with sketches and dreams was now being unveiled to the world, and the weight of that moment was not lost on him. The "Duke" car represented more than just a mechanical creation; it was a testament to his resilience, a celebration of his triumph over adversity, and a declaration of the power of dreams.

The venue buzzed with a symphony of voices - whispers of admiration, gasps of awe, and excited chatter that filled the air. The "Duke" car, draped in a shimmering cloth, stood as a centrepiece of anticipation. The cloth was a veil that concealed the culmination of countless hours of dedication, passion, and hard work.

Duke's friends - Julia, Abram, and Merriam - stood beside him, their presence a source of comfort and support. They had witnessed the journey first-hand, and their belief in him had been an unwavering constant through all the challenges. Their smiles and encouraging words served as a reminder that he was not alone in this moment.

As Duke stepped forward to address the crowd, his voice trembled with a mixture of nerves and excitement. He spoke not just about the "Duke" car as a piece of machinery, but about the journey that had led him to this point. He shared the story of the trial, the challenges he had faced, and the unwavering support of his friends and family. The spoke of the motto - "No weapons formed against you" - and the profound significance it held.

With a deep breath and a sense of purpose, Duke signalled for the cloth to be removed. As the fabric fell away, revealing the "Duke" car in all its glory, a collective gasp swept through the crowd. The sleek curves, the aerodynamic lines, and the meticulous craftsmanship were a testament to Duke's dedication and vision. The car stood as a symbol of innovation and engineering prowess, but it also stood as a symbol of triumph.

Velocity of Hope

The unveiling was met with applause, cheers, and even a few tears. Duke's journey, marked by trials and resilience, had found its expression in the form of a car that carried the weight of his dreams. The crowd's reaction was not just a response to a mechanical creation; it was a response to a story of triumph over adversity, a journey of self-discovery, and the power of unwavering determination.

As Duke looked at the "Duke" car, now standing in the spotlight, he felt a sense of awe and humility. The dream that had taken root in his heart during his childhood had now grown into something tangible and profound. The journey had been arduous, the challenges had been formidable, but the result was a testament to the power of dreams and the resilience of the human spirit.

As the crowd continued to admire the "Duke" car, Duke's heart swelled with a mixture of emotions. He had not just unveiled a car; he had unveiled a dream. And as he stood amidst the applause and admiration, he knew that this moment was not just the end of a chapter; it was the beginning of a legacy that would inspire generations to come.

TRIUMPH OF VISION

The "Duke" car stood before the crowd, a shimmering embodiment of Duke's unwavering dedication and the culmination of his journey. Its sleek lines, innovative features, and the motto "No weapons formed against you" etched into its emblem resonated deeply with everyone present. The car was more than just a machine; it was a symbol of resilience, triumph, and the power of dreams.

Duke took the stage once more, his heart brimming with a mixture of emotions. His speech was a reflection of his journey - a journey marked by challenges, setbacks, and ultimately, triumph. His words were filled with gratitude, not only for the opportunity to design and create the "Duke" car, but also for the obstacles he had overcome and the support that had sustained him throughout.

The spoke of the trial that had tested his character and his resolve, of the friends who had stood by him, and of the family who had provided unwavering love. He acknowledged the mentors and the team at his father's company who had guided and supported him, turning his dream into a tangible reality. His speech was a tribute to the collective effort that had brought the "Duke" car to life.

Velocity of Hope

Amid applause, admiration, and the nodding heads of industry insiders, Duke's speech resonated deeply. The journey he had undertaken was not just about engineering; it was about perseverance, determination, and the capacity to rise above challenges. The car before them was not just an object; it was a testament to the power of vision and the triumph of the human spirit.

As Duke concluded his speech, the applause swelled, filling the venue with a resounding affirmation of his achievements. The dreamer had become the architect of his own success, and his journey had inspired those around him. The "Duke" car had taken on a life of its own, carrying with it the weight of Duke's story and the significance of his journey.

As the crowd mingled around the car, admiring its design and innovative features, Duke looked on with a sense of fulfillment. The challenges he had faced had not deterred him; they had fueled his determination.

The setbacks he had encountered had not broken him; they had only strengthened his resolve. And the dream he had nurtured since childhood had not remained a distant fantasy; it had become a tangible reality that stood proudly before him.

The "Duke" car was a triumph of vision - a vision that had been shaped by adversity, guided by determination, and brought to life by the power of dreams. Its unveiling was not just a celebration of a mechanical creation; it was a celebration of human potential, of the capacity to overcome obstacles, and of the unwavering belief that dreams could be turned into reality.

As the event came to a close, and the crowd slowly dispersed, Duke's heart was filled with a sense of accomplishment that words could hardly capture. The "Duke" car had become more than just a dream; it had become a legacy, an inspiration, and a testament to the triumph of the human spirit. And as he looked at the car one last time, Duke knew that his journey was far from over; it was just beginning, with the road ahead brimming with new dreams and endless possibilities.

LEGACY FORGED

The success of the "Duke" car marked not just a moment of triumph, but the forging of a lasting legacy. Duke's journey, which had begun with a childhood dream and led to the creation of a masterpiece, had transformed him into a source of inspiration for generations to come.

Duke's story became a beacon of hope, a testament to the power of perseverance and the strength of the human spirit. His journey from a dreamer with a passion for cars to a visionary engineer who had turned his dreams into reality resonated deeply with those who heard it. It was a reminder that even in the face of adversity, dreams could be realized through unwavering determination and resilience.

The "Duke" car stood as a physical representation of Duke's legacy. Its sleek lines, innovative features, and the motto that encapsulated his journey were a testament to his dedication and vision. Every time someone laid eyes on the car, they were reminded that dreams were not confined to the realm of fantasy; they could be brought to life through hard work, perseverance, and the refusal to give up.

Duke's journey became a story shared in classrooms, boardrooms, and living rooms alike. His triumph over challenges served as a source of motivation for those facing their own obstacles. His journey from adversity to success became a blueprint for turning setbacks into stepping stones, doubts into determination, and dreams into reality.

The legacy Duke had forged went beyond the "Duke" car itself. It extended to the lives he touched, the minds he inspired, and the aspirations he ignited. His story became a catalyst for change, an agent of empowerment, and a source of courage for those who dared to dream.

As Duke looked back on his journey, he couldn't help but feel a sense of pride, not just in his achievements, but in the legacy he had created. The trials he had faced, the challenges he had conquered, and the dreams he had pursued had all contributed to a story that was now part of a greater narrative of resilience and hope.

The "Duke" car continued to inspire awe and admiration, serving as a constant reminder of the journey that had brought it into existence. And with each passing day, as the legacy Duke had forged continued to spread, the impact of his story grew, inspiring others to dare to dream, to overcome obstacles, and to believe in the possibility of creating something extraordinary from the seeds of a simple dream.

As Duke looked at the "Duke" car, he knew that its legacy was intertwined with his own, a legacy that would live on long after he was gone. And as he contemplated the road ahead, he was filled with a sense of purpose - the knowledge that his journey was not just his own, but a part of a larger tapestry of human potential and the relentless pursuit of dreams.

A NEW CHAPTER

As the sun set on the chapter of Duke's life that had been defined by challenges, triumphs, and the creation of the "Duke" car, a new chapter awaited him, brimming with possibilities. Graduation day arrived, marking the end of his university journey, but also heralding the beginning of a fresh adventure that awaited him beyond the campus gates.

With his degree in engineering firmly in hand and a heart full of dreams that had been refined through fire, Duke stood at the threshold of the wider world. The university had been a crucible that had forged his skills, honed his abilities, and nurtured his passion. Armed with knowledge and a determination that had been tested and proven, he was ready to step out into the industry he had long aspired to leave his mark on - the automotive industry.

As he walked across the stage to receive his diploma, the cheers of his family, friends, and mentors filled the air. The applause was not just a celebration of his academic achievement; it was a recognition of the journey he had undertaken and the growth he had undergone. The trials he had faced had transformed him from a dreamer into a doer, from a hopeful individual into a visionary engineer.

The graduation ceremony marked the closing of one chapter and the opening of another. Duke's heart was a blend of nostalgia for the experiences he had shared with friends and mentors, and excitement for the challenges and opportunities that awaited him in the real world. The friendships he had formed, the lessons he had learned, and the resilience he had cultivated would continue to be his companions as he embarked on this new phase of his journey.

As Duke tossed his graduation cap into the air, it symbolized not just the culmination of his academic pursuits, but the liberation of his dreams. The cap soared skyward, a representation of the aspirations and goals that were no longer confined to the realm of the classroom. The world beyond the campus was vast and waiting, and Duke was determined to leave an indelible mark on it.

With his degree as a key and his dreams as a compass, Duke stepped forward into the uncharted territory of the professional world. The lessons he had learned, both inside and outside the classroom, would guide him as he navigated the challenges, seized the opportunities, and continued to chase after the visions that had driven him from the very beginning.

As Duke looked back one last time at the campus that had been his home for years, he did so with gratitude for the experiences that had shaped him. But his gaze was not fixed on the past; it was fixed on the horizon, where a new chapter awaited him. With determination in his step and dreams in his heart, Duke set out to make his mark on the world, ready to create a legacy that would continue to inspire for generations to come.

MERRIAM'S CHOICE

With Duke's name finally cleared and their future no longer shrouded in uncertainty, a new chapter opened in Merriam's life. The trials and challenges she had weathered alongside Duke had forged a bond between them that was unbreakable. However, as the dust settled and clarity emerged, Merriam found herself facing her own decisions and aspirations.

The journey they had shared had solidified their connection, and the love that had blossomed between them was undeniable. Yet, Merriam's heart harboured aspirations that were uniquely her own. As she gazed at the horizon of possibilities, she realized that the path she wanted to tread was a blend of her artistic talent and her deep desire to make a meaningful impact on the world.

In the wake of the tumultuous events they had faced, Merriam had discovered a renewed sense of purpose. Her artistic abilities, once confined to the realm of passion, now beckoned to be woven into something more profound. She contemplated how her talents could become a medium for change, a way to bring attention to important issues and touch hearts in ways that only art could.

Velocity of Hope

Merriam's dreams were coloured with hues of social justice and advocacy. She envisioned using her art to raise awareness about causes close to her heart - to give voice to those who were often unheard, to shine a light on injustices, and to spark conversations that could lead to meaningful change. She had witnessed first-hand the power of resilience, and she wanted to harness that power to inspire others through her creative expressions.

As she stood at this crossroads, Merriam knew that her decisions would shape not just her own future, but also the future she could build with Duke. Their love was undeniable, and their journey had bound them together in profound ways. She pondered how her dreams could align with their shared aspirations, how her creative endeavours could complement the legacy Duke was forging.

With Duke's unwavering support, Merriam embarked on a journey of her own. She sought guidance, explored opportunities, and delved into projects that melded her artistic talents with her passion for change. The bond between her and Duke remained strong, fortified by a love that had overcome trials and adversity.

In the midst of her pursuits, Merriam found herself weaving threads of inspiration into her art. Her pieces became a reflection of the journey she and Duke had undertaken - a journey of resilience, hope, and the unbreakable bond they shared. Each stroke of the brush, each creation she birthed, was infused with the spirit of their story, a story that had evolved from the darkness of doubt to the brilliance of triumph.

As she looked ahead, Merriam knew that her choice to pursue her dreams was not a divergence from their shared path, but a continuation of it. Just as Duke had transformed his dream into reality with the "Duke" car, Merriam was weaving her dreams into tangible expressions that had the power to touch hearts and minds. Their paths might take them on separate journeys, but their destinies remained intertwined in the tapestry of their love and shared experiences.

With each piece of art she created, Merriam found herself embracing not only her own aspirations, but also the profound connection she shared with Duke. Their individual dreams, woven together, created a narrative of resilience, courage, and the boundless potential of human endeavour. As they stood on the cusp of their respective futures, Merriam knew that their love story would continue to inspire, with each of them following their passions, and together, creating a legacy that defied the limits of time and circumstance.

THE WINDS OF CHANGE

As Duke stepped into the professional world, ready to make his mark on the automotive industry, Joseph and Tina stood on the side-lines, watching with a mixture of pride and nostalgia. Their son's journey had been one of trials and triumphs, and now, as they witnessed his first steps into this new chapter, they couldn't help but reflect on their own remarkable journey.

The automotive business that Joseph and Tina had built, starting from humble beginnings, had not only survived the tests of time but had thrived. The legacy they had painstakingly crafted had weathered storms and challenges, growing into a symbol of their resilience, determination, and unwavering belief. Their success was not just measured in financial terms; it was a testament to the power of dreams nurtured through hard work, dedication, and a willingness to adapt to the winds of change.

As they looked back on the years, Joseph and Tina marvelled at how far they had come. The journey had not been without its share of obstacles and uncertainties, but their unwavering commitment to their vision had guided them through the darkest of times. The automotive business had grown from a small shop into a thriving enterprise, and each success, each milestone, had been a triumph over adversity.

The trials they had faced had tested their mettle, and the setbacks had taught them valuable lessons. They had navigated economic fluctuations, industry shifts, and the inevitable challenges that come with running a business. But their shared determination, their ability to adapt, and their unbreakable bond had carried them through.

And now, with Duke's success as an engineer and the unveiling of the "Duke" car, Joseph and Tina felt a deep sense of accomplishment. Their legacy felt complete, a story of dreams that had been realized through hard work, perseverance, and an unyielding belief in the power of possibility. Duke's journey was a testament to the values they had instilled in him, and his achievements were a reflection of the legacy they had cultivated.

As they watched their son confidently step into the professional world, they knew that his path was intertwined with their own. Duke carried not only his own dreams but also the dreams of generations that had come before him. The automotive business was more than just a source of income; it was a reflection of their family's resilience and a tribute to the legacy they had built.

Joseph and Tina felt a deep sense of gratitude for the opportunities they had seized, the challenges they had overcome, and the love that had guided them through it all. Their story was a reminder that dreams were not confined to the realm of fantasy; they could be brought to life through hard work, unwavering belief, and a willingness to adapt to the changing tides.

As they looked at Duke, their hearts swelled with pride. The winds of change had blown them in unexpected directions, but they had weathered them all, emerging stronger and more united. Their journey was far from over, but as they stood together, watching their son embark on his own path, they knew that their legacy was secure - a legacy of dreams fulfilled, challenges conquered, and the unbreakable bonds of family that had carried them through it all.

JULIA'S PATH

As Duke's journey continued to unfold, the spotlight also shifted to Julia, a key figure in the trio that had stood by his side through thick and thin. Julia's own path had taken shape, leading her down unexpected but exciting avenues that merged her fascination with technology and her passion for cars.

Julia's affinity for coding and technology had been evident from an early age. The intricate dance of algorithms and the potential to shape the future through lines of code had always captivated her. As she pursued her studies in computer science, her path intersected with the world of automotive software innovations - a realm where her expertise could revolutionize the driving experience.

With each new project and innovation, she embarked upon, Julia discovered the immense impact technology could have on the automotive industry. Her work wasn't just about coding; it was about creating seamless and intuitive interfaces, enhancing safety through automation, and ushering in a new era of connected vehicles. The possibilities were limitless, and Julia found herself at the forefront of a technological revolution.

Velocity of Hope

As she navigated the ever-evolving landscape of technology and automotive engineering, Julia faced challenges that tested her mettle. The road was not without its bumps, but Julia's determination was unwavering. She found herself drawn to projects that melded her expertise with her passion for cars, each challenge a canvas upon which she could leave her mark.

Her work had a ripple effect, touching the lives of drivers and passengers alike. Whether it was designing user-friendly interfaces that made driving safer or developing systems that optimized fuel efficiency, Julia's contributions were shaping the future of transportation. Her journey wasn't just about writing lines of code; it was about harnessing the power of technology to redefine the driving experience.

Julia's dedication and expertise were noticed and acknowledged by industry leaders. She found herself at the centre of collaborations that united engineers, designers, and tech enthusiasts, all driven by a common goal - to revolutionize the automotive industry. The projects she worked on were bridges between her passion for coding and her love for cars, reminding her that every challenge she tackled was a step toward creating a better future.

As Julia's journey continued, her path intersected with Duke's once more. Their shared passion for cars and their expertise in different realms created opportunities for collaboration. Their separate journeys had taken them down unique avenues, but their convergence was a testament to the strength of their bond and the power of shared aspirations.

In the ever-changing world of technology and automotive engineering, Julia's path was a reflection of her determination to push boundaries and explore uncharted territories. She was a pioneer, a visionary whose work was leaving an indelible mark on the industry she was so passionate about. And as she looked ahead, she knew that her journey was far from over; it was a continuous exploration of innovation, challenges, and the limitless potential of technology to transform the way we experience the world of cars.

ABRAM'S EPIPHANY

The trials and tribulations that had shaken Duke's world had a profound impact on Abram as well. The weight of the events they had endured had sparked an epiphany within him - a realization of the fragility of life and the urgency of pursuing one's dreams without hesitation.

As the events unfolded, Abram found himself grappling with the harsh reality that life was unpredictable and fleeting. The loss of their friend, the accusations that had hung over Duke, and the subsequent triumph of truth had stirred something deep within Abram's heart. The stark reminder that life could change in an instant prompted him to revaluate his own journey.

With a newfound sense of purpose, Abram embarked on a journey of self-discovery. He was determined to seize every opportunity, to explore his passions with a vigor he had never experienced before. The mechanical prowess and ingenuity that had always been a part of him became the driving force behind his pursuit of dreams.

Abram's journey led him down unexpected avenues. He found himself embracing challenges that showcased his mechanical skills, problem-solving abilities, and a thirst for innovation. Whether it was rebuilding engines, designing prototypes, or breathing new life into old machines, Abram's endeavours were a testament to his commitment to making the most of his talents.

His newfound sense of purpose didn't just stop at mechanical endeavours. Abram recognized that life was a tapestry woven with diverse threads, and he was determined to explore every colour. He delved into hobbies, interests, and creative pursuits he had once brushed aside. Photography, music, and even culinary experiments became outlets for his creativity and a means to explore the world in all its vibrant hues.

As Abram's journey of self-discovery unfolded, he found himself not just chasing dreams, but chasing a version of himself he had always wanted to become. The camaraderie of his friendship with Duke, Julia, and Merriam continued to be a source of strength and inspiration. Their shared experiences had forged a bond that was unbreakable, and their journeys, though distinct, were interconnected by the common thread of growth and self-realization.

With each challenge conquered and each dream pursued, Abram's epiphany evolved into a way of life. The lessons he had learned from the past had become guiding stars, reminding him to embrace life's uncertainties and to turn challenges into opportunities. He had witnessed the transformational power of resilience, and he was determined to embody that power in every aspect of his life.

As Abram's mechanical prowess and creative endeavours continued to intersect, he found himself on a path that was uniquely his own. The epiphany he had experienced propelled him forward, serving as a reminder to seize every moment, to chase every dream, and to celebrate the journey, no matter where it led.

And so, as Abram's story unfolded, it became a testament to the beauty of self-discovery, the importance of pursuing passions, and the power of friendship to inspire growth and change. His journey was a symphony of determination and dreams, a melody that resonated with the essence of life itself.

THE ROAD AHEAD

With his degree in engineering firmly in hand and a heart brimming with aspirations, Duke stood at the threshold of his professional journey. The road ahead was an intricate tapestry woven with challenges, opportunities, and the promise of bringing his dreams to life. As he ventured into the automotive industry, he knew that the path would be both demanding and rewarding, a test of his skills, creativity, and resilience.

The world of automotive engineering was a realm of constant evolution, where technology, design, and innovation intersected. Duke was acutely aware of the intricacies of the industry, the shifting dynamics of consumer preferences, and the relentless drive to push the boundaries of what was possible. He embraced the challenges with open arms, knowing that each obstacle was an opportunity to learn, adapt, and excel.

Collaboration became a cornerstone of Duke's professional journey. The realization that the most ground-breaking achievements were the result of collective efforts fueled his desire to work alongside fellow engineers, designers, and visionaries. Duke's ability to lead, listen, and contribute his unique perspective to the team allowed him to thrive in collaborative environments.

Velocity of Hope

As he delved into his work, Duke's dreams of creating cars that not only stirred hearts but also challenged conventions remained at the forefront of his mind. The "Duke" car had been a manifestation of his passion and innovation, and he was determined to continue pushing the envelope. Each project he undertook was a canvas upon which he painted his vision, merging aesthetics, performance, and cutting-edge technology.

The road ahead was punctuated by late nights spent refining designs, brainstorming with colleagues, and tirelessly seeking solutions to complex engineering puzzles. Duke's commitment to excellence drove him to persevere through challenges, always keeping his eye on the goal of creating vehicles that not only moved but also inspired.

In an industry marked by rapid advancements and changing landscapes, Duke's journey was a testament to adaptability. He recognized that the ability to embrace change and stay ahead of the curve was essential to success. His dedication to staying informed about emerging technologies, market trends, and sustainable practices showcased his commitment to not just designing cars, but designing the future of mobility.

And amid the hustle and bustle of the industry, Duke remained connected to his roots. The support of his family, the unwavering friendship of Julia and Abram, and the enduring love of Merriam were constants that grounded him, reminding him of the journey that had brought him to this point. Their presence was a source of inspiration, a reminder that he wasn't just creating cars; he was creating a legacy that would impact generations to come.

As Duke's journey unfolded, he held onto the lessons learned from his past - the resilience he had discovered, the friendships he had forged, and the unwavering belief in the power of dreams. The road ahead might be filled with twists and turns, but armed with his knowledge, passion, and the support of those who believed in him, Duke was ready to navigate the challenges and seize the opportunities that lay ahead. Each step was a testament to the dreamer who had evolved into a visionary engineer, ready to shape the future of the automotive world.

THE POWER OF RESILIENCE

As the years unfolded, Duke's story continued to spread like ripples in a pond, reaching hearts and minds far beyond his immediate circle. His journey, a symphony of dreams, challenges, and triumphs, resonated with people from all walks of life. Duke's story was more than just a narrative; it was a testament to the enduring power of resilience and the unwavering belief in the possibility of a better tomorrow.

The chapters of Duke's life had been marked by setbacks and hurdles, but they had also been illuminated by the unyielding light of his determination. The trials he had faced - from the accusations that shook his world to the challenges of engineering innovation - were not roadblocks but stepping stones. Each setback had been an opportunity to rise, to learn, and to evolve.

Duke's triumph over adversity was a beacon of hope for those who had faced their own trials. His story reminded them that setbacks were not destinies; they were merely chapters in a greater narrative. The power of resilience, the ability to weather storms and emerge stronger, was a theme that resonated deeply with anyone who had encountered obstacles on their own paths.

Through Duke's journey, people found solace in the knowledge that they were not alone in their struggles. They saw in him a reflection of their own aspirations and a mirror to their own dreams. His story became a reminder that dreams were worth pursuing, even in the face of adversity. Duke's unwavering belief in his vision served as an inspiration to never give up, to persevere through challenges, and to turn setbacks into catalysts for growth.

As Duke's story spread, it became a bridge between generations - a tale that parents shared with their children, teachers with their students, and friends with one another. It was a story that transcended boundaries, uniting people through a shared understanding of the human experience. Duke's journey was a reminder that life was a journey of twists and turns, of highs and lows, and that the power to shape one's destiny lay within each individual.

Duke's resilience wasn't just a personal trait; it was a philosophy that he had woven into the fabric of his life. It was a reminder that the pursuit of dreams was an act of courage, an embrace of challenges, and a declaration of hope. His journey was a testament to the fact that resilience wasn't just about bouncing back; it was about evolving, growing, and emerging from the storms with a newfound strength.

As Duke's story continued to inspire, it echoed in the hearts of those who heard it. His triumphs were their triumphs, his challenges their challenges, and his unwavering belief in the future a beacon of light guiding the way. Through Duke's journey, people learned that setbacks were temporary, dreams were worth fighting for, and the power of resilience could turn even the darkest nights into the brightest dawns.

BONDS FOREVER

The quartet of Duke, Julia, Abram, and Merriam stood as a testament to the enduring power of friendship, a bond forged in the crucible of challenges and triumphs. As their lives continued to unfold, each carving their unique paths, their connection remained unbreakable - a thread woven through the tapestry of their individual stories.

Time had a way of melding relationships, and the quartet's friendship had only grown stronger with the passing years. They had navigated the complexities of life together, weathering storms, celebrating victories, and finding solace in one another's company. Their shared experiences had etched a deep imprint on their hearts, shaping them in profound and unexpected ways.

Even as their journeys diverged, Duke, Julia, Abram, and Merriam continued to cherish the moments that had brought them together. Their bond was a reminder of the power of human connection, a lifeline that had seen them through the darkest nights and the brightest days. The challenges they had faced had not fractured their friendship; instead, they had fortified it, binding them together with an unbreakable thread of shared memories.

Velocity of Hope

Duke's journey as an engineer had led him to shape the automotive landscape with his innovations and dreams. Julia's fusion of technology and automotive had paved the way for ground-breaking advancements, merging two worlds that were once seen as disparate. Abram's pursuit of dreams had taken him on unexpected paths, each one a testament to his resilience and determination. And Merriam's artistic journey had intertwined with her desire to make a difference, creating a tapestry of compassion and creativity.

Their paths may have taken them to different corners of the world, but their hearts remained interconnected. Duke's successes were celebrated by Julia, Abram, and Merriam, just as their triumphs were felt by him. The quartet's bond was a source of unwavering support, a reminder that no matter the distance, their friendship could bridge any gap.

Through the years, they continued to create new memories - road trips, reunions, and shared milestones. Their lives had evolved, their dreams had grown, but the essence of their connection remained unchanged. The quartet had learned the true value of friendship - a lifeline that offered comfort, guidance, and companionship even when life took unexpected turns.

As Duke's automotive innovations continued to shape the future, as Julia's technology-infused creations pushed boundaries, as Abram's resilience transformed challenges into stepping stones, and as Merriam's artistry inspired change, their bond stood as a reminder that life's journey was meant to be shared. Their stories were woven together, a tapestry of dreams realized through resilience, creativity, and unwavering friendship.

And so, as the quartet ventured into new chapters, they carried with them the lessons they had learned from one another. Their friendship was a beacon of hope, a living testament to the beauty of human connection. Through challenges and triumphs, setbacks and successes, their bond remained a constant, a reminder that some bonds were meant to last a lifetime and beyond - a treasure they held close as they continued their individual journeys while forever cherishing the bonds that had shaped their lives.

REFLECTIONS

In the quiet moments of solitude, Duke often found himself immersed in reflections of his journey - a journey that had taken him from the depths of doubt to the heights of triumph, from a young dreamer sketching designs in his childhood room to an engineer who had turned those designs into reality. His path had been a labyrinth of highs and lows, each twist and turn leaving an indelible mark on his heart and soul.

The journey had not been without its challenges, and Duke carried with him the scars of adversity. But those scars were not signs of weakness; they were badges of strength, reminders of the battles he had fought and the victories he had earned. The moments of doubt and darkness had not defined him; they had propelled him forward, shaping him into the person he had become.

The reflections carried with them a tapestry of memories - the innocence of childhood, the passion of youth, the trials of adversity, and the triumphs of resilience. Duke saw his journey as a mosaic of experiences, each fragment contributing to the larger picture of his life's narrative. From the seed of a childhood dream to the bloom of a masterful creation, every step had been a thread in the tapestry of his destiny.

Through it all, Duke had learned the value of persistence, the strength of community, and the beauty of embracing change. He had learned that dreams were not mere fantasies; they were blueprints of possibility waiting to be crafted. He had learned that the road to success was not linear; it was a winding path that required resilience, adaptability, and an unyielding belief in oneself.

And as he looked back on his journey, Duke was filled with gratitude for the people who had walked beside him. His parents, Joseph and Tina, had been pillars of support, showing him the power of unwavering love and belief. Julia, Abram, and Merriam had been more than friends; they had been his comrades in arms, his fellow travellers in the quest for dreams.

Duke's reflections also carried the wisdom of experience - the understanding that life was a canvas waiting to be painted with vibrant strokes of purpose, passion, and persistence. The scars of adversity were not marks of defeat; they were symbols of growth, a testament to the resilience of the human spirit.

And so, in those moments of quiet contemplation, Duke found solace in the journey he had undertaken. Every setback had been a setup for a comeback, every challenge an opportunity for growth. He had emerged not unscathed, but stronger, wiser, and more determined than ever. His reflections were a reminder that life was a symphony of moments, each note contributing to the melody of one's existence.

With a heart full of gratitude and a mind brimming with memories, Duke looked ahead to the future, knowing that the journey was far from over. The road stretched onward, a canvas waiting to be painted with new dreams, new challenges, and new triumphs. And as he continued to chase the horizon, Duke carried with him the lessons etched into his heart - those dreams were worth pursuing, that resilience could turn setbacks into stepping stones, and that reflection was a compass that guided the way forward.

FULL CIRCLE

In the grand tapestry of time, Duke's story had come full circle - a narrative that had transformed a dreamer into the embodiment of his dreams, where passion had given birth to legacy, and the journey had become a beacon of inspiration for all who encountered it. The threads of his life's journey had woven a masterpiece that spanned continents and hearts, leaving an indelible mark on the world.

As the years unfurled their wings, Johannesburg stood as the place where Duke's story had begun - a city that had witnessed the birth of his dreams, the trials that had tested his spirit, and the triumphs that had elevated his soul. Amidst the bustling streets and the cacophony of life, Duke's motto, "No weapons formed against you," resonated like a timeless melody, a declaration of victory over adversity, a testament to the enduring strength of the human spirit.

The dreamer who had once filled the pages of his notebook with sketches of cars had now become the fulfilled, a visionary engineer who had turned his dreams into reality. His path had been a symphony of determination, resilience, and unwavering belief, each note contributing to the crescendo of his success. The obstacles that had stood in his way had become the stepping stones that propelled him forward.

Duke's legacy radiated beyond the confines of the automotive industry. It was a story that spoke to the hearts of those who dared to dream, who faced challenges head-on, and who found the courage to rise after each fall. His journey had become a source of inspiration, a reminder that dreams were not merely distant stars but were within reach of those willing to chase them with passion and perseverance.

The legacy Duke had crafted was a mirror reflecting the power of the human spirit. It was a story of triumph over adversity, of turning setbacks into setups for success, and of shaping one's destiny through determination and hard work. The "Duke" car had become more than a vehicle; it was a vessel carrying the essence of a dreamer's heart and the motto that had guided his steps.

And so, as the final chapters of Duke's story were written, the pages turned with a sense of fulfillment. The dreamer had realized his dreams, the passion had ignited a fire that would continue to burn, and the journey had become a map guiding others toward their own horizons. In Johannesburg, where it had all begun, the echoes of Duke's journey reverberated through time, reminding all who heard it that no weapon formed against them could extinguish the flame of their dreams.

Duke's story was a legacy that lived on, a testament to the human spirit's ability to transcend limitations and transform challenges into triumphs. The dreamer had come full circle, leaving behind a trail of inspiration for generations to come, a legacy woven into the very fabric of history. And as the world continued to turn, Duke's story remained a beacon of hope, a reminder that within every heart beats the potential to create, to overcome, and to come full circle - a journey that never truly ends, but instead transforms into new beginnings.

EPILOGUE: ECHOES OF DREAMS

The passage of time is a tapestry woven with the threads of countless stories, each contributing to the rich mosaic of human experience. Duke's story, a journey of dreams, adversity, and triumph, had left an indelible mark on the world. The epilogue of his tale brings us to a moment of reflection, a pause to gaze upon the legacy he had carved.

Years had slipped through the fingers of time since Duke's triumph over adversity. The "Duke" car stood as a monument to his determination, an emblem of resilience that continued to inspire all who beheld it. The automotive industry had been transformed by his innovations, his spirit echoing in every engine's roar and every sleek design.

Julia had carved her own path in the realm of technology-infused automotive advancements, pushing boundaries and creating a bridge between the digital world and the world of machines. Abram had embraced challenges as opportunities, leaving his imprint on mechanical marvels that left the world in awe. Merriam had found her own way to inspire change, marrying her artistic gifts with her desire to make a difference.

Their paths had diverged, yet their bonds remained steadfast. They had become living proof that friendships forged in the crucible of trials could stand the test of time. Duke's parents, Joseph and Tina, had seen their son's legacy flourish, their hearts swelling with pride as they witnessed the impact he had made.

Johannesburg had not forgotten the dreamer who had emerged from its streets. Duke's motto, "No weapons formed against you," had become a rallying cry, a beacon of hope for those who faced challenges. The echoes of his story resonated in the air, a reminder that dreams were not just ethereal fantasies, but seeds waiting to be nurtured.

The epilogue finds Duke at a crossroads once more. The years had brought him fulfillment, but the yearning for new horizons remained. As he gazed upon the open road, he felt a familiar fire kindling within. The dreamer's heart had not grown dormant; it still beat with the rhythm of aspiration.

With a heart full of gratitude for the journey he had undertaken, Duke set forth on a new adventure. The road stretched ahead, a canvas awaiting new dreams to be painted upon it. The legacy he had built would forever be a part of him, guiding his steps and whispering encouragement in his ear.

And so, as the final pages of this tale close, the legacy of Duke's journey continues to unfold. It is a story that reminds us all that dreams are not confined to the realm of sleep, but can shape the world when embraced with determination. It is a story that declares that challenges are not the end, but opportunities for growth. It is a story that echoes through time, a testament to the human spirit's power to overcome and create.

The epilogue invites us to reflect on our own journeys, to ask ourselves what dreams lie within us waiting to be awakened, and to remember that the journey is not linear, but a tapestry of experiences that shape us. As the sun sets on this chapter, it rises on the next, and the story continues, always full of potential, always ready to be written.

www.ingramcontent.com/pod-product-compliance
Lightning Source LLC
Chambersburg PA
CBHW021115080526
44587CB00010B/527